Conversations with a Short Circuit

By

Ferris E. Jones

ISBN: 978-81-8253-894-8

First Edition: 2022
Rs. 200/-

Cyberwit.net
HIG 45 Kaushambi Kunj, Kalindipuram
Allahabad - 211011 (U.P.) India
http://www.cyberwit.net
Tel: +(91) 9415091004
E-mail: info@cyberwit.net

Printed at Repro India Limited.

Contents

Picture

An illustrated memory
does not testify.
There are no explanations,
it proposes its reason.
It can disintegrate a mortal,
into an anguished circumstance.
Reckless.
Eyes admire you as fodder,
its sublime peacetime
pleasure.
Devotions are but a disgraceful
reprieve.

Just for Fun

Some are born with a silver spoon,
others a silver bullet.
It might be why I carry a gun.
Walk right up to the line.
Just because it is fun.

Blame is for the privileged few.
They held it tight.
No one knew.
I wake with my bride without sin.
Regret for nothing. Therefore, I win.

Pause

And I waver.
No explosion is happening.
I expect.
Still rising.
The dicing of our time jointly.
A large withdrawal from a schedule.
Acting on, calculated.
Caressed by many scribblings.
We wade in an aquarium.
Too much food and we pass.
Not adequate and we pass.
If the water becomes inactive, we pass.
An alert.
The porch light is white.
The voice of the summer children has ceased.
Empty.
A paperweight lies on my breast.
The words are cloudy.
I have lost my place.
I need the television for companionship.
It's time to sleep.
My thoughts drip.

The Dressmaker

Wealth is a relentless disguise.
A rosy light, blooming, anonymous.
Savage, strange new wallpaper.
Motionless, deceiving to the gods.
Balloons of a child.
Carry its own weather, the moon follows.
The driver knows better.
The dressmaker faults the bloat,
given as a birthday present.
Instilled over generations.
Fissures warm in a scheme of unbalanced,
thin conditions.
Display a human in disrepair.

224 - Today, Tomorrow and Forever

An old Ford pickup pulls off the highway. The driver shifts the car into park, takes a Pepsi and a bottle of vodka from a grocery bag. The door opens, *Come Sail Away* by Styx blares. He dumps out half the bottle of Pepsi and fills it back up with vodka. He guzzles half the Pepsi, takes out two bottles of Sprite, dumps them both out and refills them to the rim with vodka.

He places them back into the bag and shuts the truck's door.

Hazy tail lights and dust as he pulls back onto the highway.

West.

A nurse walks the long empty hallway, stops and opens the door for room number two-twenty-four. A man with one arm is asleep in the bed.

She pulls a drinking straw from his left hand and tosses it onto the nightstand where two large bottles of Sprite and a pill bottle rest next to a cell phone.

She turns to leave, the man's eyes open. He reaches across his body and takes back the straw, putting it under the blanket. The Sprite bottles have inched closer to the bed.

It's 11:00 PM. The nurse is making her rounds. She opens the door to room 224. It's quiet and dark except for the small light above the bed. On the nightstand are two empty bottles of Sprite.

A straw is sticking out of one bottle. The caps are resting on the bed next to poorly written note.

I love you-224

Today, tomorrow and forever.

The nurse takes the sleeping man's pulse.

He has passed.

Bigfoot Prints in The White House Rose Garden

Folklore, Democracy fathered.
Fairness and peace, molested, slaughtered.
A Pathless emperor billows,
Weak and stupid, he still bellows.

Our minds free, welcomed, fluttered, huddled,
A hunger for white roses, troubled.
Ugly, deep were his wheeling steps.
Unaware of the prints and depths.

I hope they made a plaster cast,
To show the world, preserve the past.
Display the ape-like feature,
To become history's teacher.

Redemption Blues

Lawd, let the man redeem himself
I beg you lawd, let the man redeem himself
He's done grieved his injured mind
He's done abandoned the devil's kind
Lawd, let the man redeem himself

Let him know of heavens intention
Let him know of heavens intention
He's done removed himself of drink
He's done crawled on his knees from the brink
Lawd, let the man redeem himself

Please lawd
Please lawd
Please lawd, let the man redeem himself

Duty

It's not the duty of man
to sustain an unjust government,
to applaud and entertain the few
that count; and discard souls.

Unjust laws must amend thoughts,
and encourage violence to breath.
Be deliberate and contemplate a
government's death and resurrection.

Government Shutdown

Lay a wreath
Buy a pine box
Raise your own flag
Let grandma fold it,
Nicely now!
It's a small burden
Let down in death
The County has failed you
No twenty-one-gun salute
Save your bullets
Storm the Congress
Put them on trial
For treason.

The Wicked Witch
(Johnny's Poem)

Memories are but a slide show caught in a tornado.
With a pour, of both joy and pain that buckles the gate-
once held the pieces of our life.

The wicked witch will fly past us all at some point!!

Laughing at our past and begging for our future.
The mind will flash of friendships; and love,
Both forgotten, lost and continued for decades.
These cannot be taken by the wind of the soulless.

They will be with you when you stand at the doorstep.
Gazing at the sentry with surprise, as he knows your heart
Which is judged by how much you are loved.

a bible keeping up the window

the rugged make do, devise. receive from the expansive sky's release. mariners star gaze. design as you frolic. produce a gust, a direction to moderate the chamber. seek surroundings, thrust aside from yourself. capture the world's substances. adopt them as required.

a hotel bible opens quietly. its plan rests in your palm. its value occurs in improving wisdom. there are higher processes to recover god. see clearly from the free window afforded. prosper with the thorns. chant with the grasses.

Finish

It demands no dislike of your start.
Be delivery by growler or tart.
Birth may prove a Caesar.
Caressed as a deceiver.

A petition for a path.
Walk floods of wrath.
Execute a measure of violence.
Accept a promise of silence.

Secrete a pearl of Apelles.
Sing the battles of Achilles.
It's the finish, the day.
You are required to sway.

Cycle

Delivered into the garden.
Sunflowers rock the sky.
A signature of love lies
in the meadow of blue eyes.
The waft rises in life.
Declare wisdom refuses
to see to the stars.
It's death, blackness.
The points of floundering
in normality. Dealing with
creation and its result.
Times, many experiences
with brief nights. Views of history,
announced. The cycle of the earth
bears notice, gazes upward.

A Nicker without a Companion

He trotted from the surf.
A probe, repeatedly glancing back.
Foam drifts in on the moon.
The legend groans with the star.
His hair drips loneliness.
His steps invariably position back to the sea.
Rocks are rugged.
They transcend the sand.
An immense sense approaches.
It's the Satyr, not the nixie.

To be a Priest

Adorn in the fresh rush of existence.
The course twists with abundant stones.
An abrupt halt.
A sign argues,
to be a priest or a gangster.
In fever, life determined.
Neither can adequately serve.
Peyote drifts with the poet.

Ten Acres

Ten acres, soaring the esophagus of poverty.
White mountains border freedom.
Substance is bare, original.
Motion limits in view.
Swerving brings home.
White vessels of a newborn need sovereignty.

Stories will sound of hidden skeletons.
Love will ascend from the grave, tending.
It was of his design.
A gathering will commemorate the fragmented pieces.
Set forth a direction.
Death comes to generations of deaf ears.

The Window

Ecstasies live in its inflection,
Vastness kneels, humming
Along with the sapling.
Spilling into fantasies,
As a reservoir, pleasant
With a spirit.

Pathetic

I was consistently pathetic.
But what an experience he was.
Over and over cosmetic.
The forests had overhang.
The ball fled into the basket.
Words of a boomerang.
Young were the sentiments.
Polite features examined,
fondling compliments.

Each Night

This bridewell enjoys its captive.
Spilling barriers of age.
No codes to the door.

Hypnotic the ice-blink entombs.
The green eye violates the blue eye.
Bacchus jabs at the eyelids, seething.

A burst of Peter Pan rushing to reach God.
He wavers, inches.
A gate opens.

Chunks of grass surrounded by dirt.
The images reflected.
It cracks the limousine window.

Begat

The painter, contentious.
The poet, broken.
Taking images.
Decayed dozing in the drizzle.
Swallowed by a madman,
his pages slip apart.
Word's swimming, volatile.
Belief in the vibrations of his head,
synthetic.
Norms constructed by formulating,
youthful.
Pearls, elegant stubbles
at a dartboard.
Thoughts, begat thought.
Thought begat thoughts.

Returning

Spoils of an education,
fog along the shore.
Basking daily,
worshipping for more.

Fraternity of fanfare,
inflection spent on years.
Caves of past friendships,
spoiling all the fears.

To return as a diamond,
a future climb, aroused.
Hovering above the past,
witnessing those whom caroused.

Sonny

Let's stall a moment. My best friend's name is not Sonny. We found each other in the cold of 1977. There were 12 days below zero. The longest unbroken string of sub-freezing weather in Philadelphia history. My thirteenth birthday in a hotel room. A surrounding of its time. Orange drapes looked out at cold doom. Stunned, I walked to school. People called me *California Smog Boy*. My father's advice; hit the next person in the face. I did. For Sonny, I was the cool kid from California. The girls paid consideration to us; we became indivisible.

We adopted the dreaming years. Rite of passage screamed. We took our first girlfriends to a dance. Cruised in my 1969 Mustang. Played high school football and baseball. How to spend our millions? Time can shatter the glass. The repairman came in the summer of 1984. Sonny treated every day as a marble god. Robert, a remarkable artist, had a swimming pool. Our oracle. Spent our days seeking direction. The best summer of my life.

Years, trips to Philly. Sonny appeared to the west coast. Both drinking heavily. His first round of golf. Robert faded away, bright, divorced. John was in Butte, Montana. Joe was in Florida. Hopped on airplanes. Three days of fishing. Together after thirty-five years. I had stopped drinking. John's household was marvelous. Joe owes a business. It's my honor. Sonny's comments are living. He had Hepatitis and liver disease. Tell no one. I concurred. I was disguising the reason I had quit drinking.

(One average, COVID-19 Monday night I received a text message from Sonny).

—— I wanted to say goodbye (sorry it was in a text). I was okay with my childhood, the odd man out w/my siblings made it a better social life. I thoroughly enjoyed my wild and crazy bachelor life that I was lucky enough to experience. Dating my wife was outstanding! Nobody ever made me laugh as much as she (that's why I married her). My friends are all controlled by their wives, corporate America controls my livelihood and I've just grown tired of trying to live my life and always being shot down. W/my health, what do I have to gain by sticking around? More continuous disappointment? I'm done, I'm tired, I just want to head off to the unknown, maybe there is truly something better out there for me? I just know I'm tired of waiting on nothing to look forward to. We've had a lot of good times/memories, thanks for accepting me for being me after all these years. Thanks for being my best friend!!!!! Wishing you receive all that life has to offer–in the manner that you had hoped & strived for.

—— Dude, that was an accidentally sent......

——Oh, I got some explaining to do

(Then I responded)

—— Yeah, you sounded like a suicidal Unabomber.

(Sonny)

——Truthfully, that's where I'm at.... My intentions were to have it on my phone if I don't wake up tomorrow.

—— at least someone would know how I felt. That person was you.

(Me)

—— Well. I'm glad you chose me. But don't do nothing crazy. You need to stick around for a trip next summer if this stupid virus goes away. I'm with your thought brother no matter what happens.

(Sonny)

—— I honestly don't know if the whisky & what little pills, we had in the house will get me where I'm going, but if it doesn't, I'll text u in the morning. Don't dwell or panic on my actions, just try to understand. I'm sorry for the incidental text, please don't judge me wrong.

(Me)

——You are my best friend and I would never judge you. You never judged me when everybody else wrote me off. Hope to talk to you tomorrow.

(Sonny)

—— Me too. I know my wife still loves me, and it truly is until death do us part. Thanks.

(Me)

—— Love ya brother.

I didn't get another text that night. Can you believe it in the middle of a pandemic? There were lots of messages being sent out each night. I didn't sleep. Prayed when I don't pray. I have no right to judge. I have not earned it. Love forced no action. He would do the same for me.

(In the morning I received one more text from Sonny).

—— I'm still here. I don't know what was going thru my mind last night. If I didn't see the note, I probably wouldn't have gotten back to you. Fortunately, this wasn't a pre-planned act. I'm sick as hell going back to bed, going to take the day off and truly think about what's going on. Sorry for putting u thru this….

(Me)

—— It's all good with me. I'm just glad to hear you are still here.

(The next weekend I sent him pictures of the fish I caught on my camping trip with my family. He laughed at the size of the fish).

Become

Alone, in silence.
The multi-glows of children
pedal in their futures.
It dropped.
The five-petal ruffled cluster.
The earth preserved
its importance.
Change, though turning,
protected in color.
World as we need it.
What is; becomes.
What becomes; is.
Old bones remember.
Smile.
The bite of many ages'
crawls.
Finds its home.
Rests tranquil for the night.

The King Is Dead

The strip,
he commands.
Devine madness of grime.
There.
The myth never expires.
Children never stray.
Cars explode.
Bodies limp.
Produced people.
Hearts implode.
Blood smears,
stains the surface.
Blocks the cracks.
Whores work hungry.
He feels nothing.
A poor junkie.

Our Slowest Day

Light flows through
our slowest day.
Understanding the ghosts
of civilizations,
sacrifices, witnesses.
Each year.
Without reactions for many.
We made phones clap and
the judgement of men occurs.
The apparatus spinning.
The barbarian is hot, cornered.
Desperate.
Do not examine
the nature of others.
We cannot pursue them.
Clarity should be immortal.
Many move privately.
Others take pains
to realize the barbarian.
We are as they are.
We were as they were.
Wish them completely.

Natural Creature

The poet is a natural creature.
Often relive everything.
Forgive most.
They recall the hour's
life lied, and calculate
the times inside, they died.

Nothing New Today

Destiny lumbers.
Corporate America's call girl can't speak.
She is on sabbatical.
Two weeks of grotesque nostalgia.
Dissolve the camouflage.
Start the invitation.
Bring a friend's ceremony to age.
Return, the amiable void of starvation.
Sit level, slimy god.
Beg, ghostly figure.
Roar, and dispatch him.

It's Too Hot (6/26/21)

Façade, avoiding the lord.
The infinite declares precise, gentle.
It's a code among us invited.
No token, merely a breath is required.
Blame the ancestors,
the transitions are slaying us.
Air is throbbing, coarse.
Meditation is exhausted.
Automation is how we notice God.
Passengers in space,
search out a window.
They cannot see the sparking,
vacuum that awaits.
Vessels wander effortlessly,
and their presence is as he is.

The Visit

Center stage, CARL *is donning a Chicago Cubs world series champions sweatshirt and hat. He staggers through a set of cemetery gates. A cigarette dangles from his mouth as he struggles to hold an open beer, the remnants of a twelve pack and two bouquets of flowers.*

Stage left and stage right are lined with rows of headstones. A clear path separates the two sides.

CARL

Speaking out loud. Are you freaking kidding me? I forgot this place has a black side and a white side. *Loudly* Where is the alcoholic side? *Lowers his voice.* I want my own side. Maybe there should be a white alcoholic side and a black alcoholic side. His *voice rises again.* How about a gay alcoholic side and a straight alcoholic side?

Stage right. CARL *begins to walk among the grave sites and stops to look down to read one of the headstones. He spills some beer and begins to laugh.*

CARL (cont.)

Speaking out loud. Violet Huckabee? Who in the hell would name their daughter Violet? He *Pauses*. Ah, she was born in 1891 never mind.

CARL *stumbles a bit, then walks to the next plot and places a bouquet of flowers on it. Without speaking, he flashes the peace sign then turns and walks a couple of grave sites further.*

CARL stops and stares down at one of the headstones. Then he drops the 12 pack of beer, kneels and places the flowers on the grave.

CARL (cont.)

Speaking out loud. Hey EMZ. Remember camping and talking about when Grandma died and I quoted a poem by *Mary Frye*? "Do not stand at my grave and cry; I am not there; I did not die". He *pauses.* So, I just figured I would kneel and cry instead. That, plus I don't want to spill my beer. I just poured one for your homie or neighbor over there. I know you're not normally here, but since I am, I knew you would come back so I could talk to you. Just like when we were little, remember? Always together. We will be together again someday I'm sure of that. Hey, the super bowl is tomorrow. Since you died on super bowl Sunday, watching the game is just not the same. But this year Lady Gaga is doing the half time show. *Pauses briefly.* I don't think she was even popular yet when you died. You would love her though. She is a big supporter of gay rights. The funny thing is that when she first got popular the joke was, she was really a dude. *Chuckles a bit.* Oh, also, gay marriage is now legal in the United States. I think some of your friends have even gotten married. I see their pictures and comments on *Facebook* sometimes. Remember that time we got drunk and went down to the courthouse and tried to get a marriage license for you and Sam. The look on that chick's face when she realized I really was a minister was awesome. She had no Idea that *Universal Life Church* makes anybody who answers their ad in the last page of *The Inquirer* a minister. That didn't really work out as planned, but it was funny anyway.

CARL, *reaches over and pulls out a beer and sets it next to the flowers.*

*CARL (*cont.*)*

Speaking out loud. Here, I brought you a *Miller Lite.* You know I'm a *Coors* man myself, but I figured for old time's sake we should have another beer together.

CARL, *leans over and opens the beer he just set down for* EMILY.

CARL (cont.)

Speaking out loud. I got you some flowers too.

Entering stage left is CARETAKER. *He is holding a trash bag and picking up trash. He starts to wipe down some of the headstones when he glances over and recognizes CARL. He slowly walks over to him.*

He has a large set of keys dangling from a hook on his belt.

CARL *can hear him coming and glances in his direction. A slight smile appears on his face.*

CARL (cont.)

Oh, here comes your old buddy Caretaker. It's time to talk baseball or softball just like always. Ah, that's alright, I guess.

CARETAKER

Hey Carl, what's up? Did you just get into town?

CARL

Yeah. *Standing up.* I figured I would come and visit EMZ and bring her flowers. *Pointing at the grave with flowers.* You want a beer?

CARETAKER

You do know you're not supposed to be drinking in here, right? But I guess it would be worthless to try and get you to put those back in your car?

CARL

Give me a break. I'm sure you see people drinking in here all the time. Anyway, when have you ever seen me without a beer or a glass of wine in my hand?

CARETAKER

You are right about that, my friend. I remember seeing you and your buddy Wayne watching games at the park with that big old gallon jug of wine you used to drink. *Both Laughing*. You remember Tony Jackson don't you. He played center field for you guys when you played for the Royals? The year you won that big softball tournament. He came in here one time, so drunk he pissed over there. *Pointing*. Then the idiot started yelling at some kid who was stepping on the graves and almost got the crap kicked out of him by the kid's father. He was lucky I stepped in, or he might be buried right over there. *Pointing.*

CARL

Jokingly. You do mean on the black side, right? Cause, you know I can't have him over here.

CARETAKER

You're a funny guy aren't you. *Loud and slow.* Cracker ass bastard.

CARL

You almost sound like *Samuel L Jackson* in *Pulp Fiction. Laughing*. That's funny. Where's your Jheri curl?

CARETAKER

Yeah, and you're still as bald under that hat as *Bruce Willis*.

CARL

True, but chick's do love bald guys.

CARETAKER

Not the Sista's. Maybe not all of them, I guess.

CARL

That may be true my friend but that doesn't affect me much. So, you were talking about Tony earlier. Dude, I remember that weekend we won the tournament. Did you know we had to go get him out of jail that Saturday morning just so he could come and play? I don't remember how we got him out, but he was still drunk when we finally got to the field and he was passed out in the backseat the whole drive down there. Then the crazy idiot played his ass off and won the tournament MVP. EMZ was there and she just kept feeding him beers. All the while laughing her ass off as usual. The more he drank the better he played. Unbelievable. No wonder he was drafted after high school.

CARETAKER

Oh, I remember him in high school and he was one bad ass short stop. I know you were in college in Chicago when Emily played softball here in high school. But man, she sure was something to see. I swear she was in the paper every single week back in those days. She was either pitching a no hitter or hitting home runs left and right. I hear to this day she still holds like almost every school record there is. You know even after all these years that was the only time, we won state. They haven't even come close since she stopped playing. If you went into that school right now, I bet her picture is still all over them walls.

CARL

Well, she was offered a tryout with the Olympic team that year. But like the rest of us we always seem to find a way to screw the good stuff up. *Uncomfortable pause.* Remember that time we were all drinking at the Log Cabin and she called you Buckwheat because of your hair. Man, that was so freaking funny. You were so mad you called her a cracker and she didn't know what that meant. So, she went to the refrigerator and got a piece of cheese so we could have cheese and crackers to go with the wine. Do you know what she would say right now if she could? She would ask if you clean the white side of the cemetery as well as you do the black side. *Laughing.* She would also want to know where the gay side is? Plus, what if you were black and gay? Do they bury you on the black side just way in the back or what?

CARETAKER

You're still an asshole after all these years aren't you. *Pointing at Carl's shirt.* I see your team finally, after all those years won a world series. Did you get to go to any of the games?

CARL

No, but some of my friends got to go. I did watch every second of every game though. I know EMZ was watching too. She was sitting up in Heaven, drinking a Miller Lite and just smiling her ass off. That's why I wore the shirt today.

CARETAKER

And yes, to answer your question. I do clean the cracker side as well as I clean the brother and sister's side. As a matter of fact, I always make sure Emily's is especially clean. I love to look at her headstone. That's cool what you guys did, adding a baseball and bat like that. It must of cost you guys a lot of money to have it specially made like that.

CARL

It did. But at that time, money didn't mean squat to me. I even used some of my equity money from my house to pay for it as well as the funeral. *Long Pause.* Dude, I was a complete mess for a good year after that. The kids would just look at me and ask me if I was OK. I would say I'm fine, why? And they would say because you always look like you're about to cry. For about a year I think I did. I know I wasn't a very good father or husband at that time that's for sure. I really hit the sauce too. I almost lost my job and everything. You know I'm a guy who likes his booze, but that first year almost killed me. You would have thought I would have quit altogether after that, but no. I still partake of the nectar as you can plainly see. *Pointing at what's left of the 12 pack.* But anyway, about the headstone. I had it specially made by this guy in Reno and then I paid someone to have it placed here. I was going to do it myself, but I just couldn't bring myself to come back here. It's still just kills me if I think about it too much.

CARETAKER

Didn't I hear EMZ had a scholarship somewhere around here to play softball and I think basketball too right? I remember thinking she was kind of short for basketball though

CARL

That's what I meant when I mentioned always screwing things up. She went, they flew her all the to California and everything. But, just like me she only played one year. Now for me, I quit playing for a different reason. But for EMZ. *Shaking his head.* Since she was playing so far away from all her friends. She made new ones, obviously. I never met any of them. But I heard they were just out of freaking control. A bunch of serious ball playing lesbians. These gals off the field apparently did nothing but party their ass off and get in bar fights and stuff. And of course, you know Emily she had to be right in the middle of it.

CARETAKER

I still remember when you two handed out acid to the entire town and all kinds of crazy shit started happening.

CARL

That's the night I realized things that happened to her. Both of us as kids, it was just not ever going to go away. *Pausing and shaking his head.* You know after she died, I spent days, maybe even weeks on the internet? I was trying to find a couple of guys we knew when we were kids. I was going to find them and blow their heads off. I never could find them, but I'm sure they're most likely dead or in prison anyway. I figured someone probably just beat me to it. I was even looking for death records. Anything I could find on those losers. That's how messed up I was after she died.

Center stage walking through the cemetery gates is SMOKEY. *A beer in one hand and flowers in the other. He slowly walks past* CARL *and* CARTAKER. *Oblivious to their presence, he is searching for a grave site and appears to be lost. You can clearly see that the years have worn on him.*

He is wearing the typical clothes you might see an old construction worker wearing. Complete with a very old Caterpillar hat. You can clearly see the sweat stains.

He stops, pulls the hat off his head. Pulls out a handkerchief and wipes the sweat from his head and face. He fumbles to put the handkerchief into his back pocket. His arms are waving as he talks to himself.

CARETAKER

Speaking slowly. Well, I got to go. *Nodding his head in* SMOKY'S *direction.* You remember Smokey, right?

CARL

Of course, that dude is funnier than hell. EMZ loved drinking with that old fart. I'm just glad to see him. I would have figured he was dead by now as old as he is and how much he loves to drink. Man, that could be me in 30 years. Look at that he still waves his arms around when he's talking to himself. Still pulls at the hat I see. Does he still say "Okay" all the time when he talks?

CARETAKER

Oh yeah. All the time. Every now and then he comes in here. Usually drunk of course. *His voice Rising.* What is with all you guys anyway? Nobody comes in here sober anymore.

CARL

Sarcastically. What, and take all the fun out of talking to dead people. Expecting an answer is not something a sober person would expect right?

CARETAKER

Anyway, he comes in here every so often to sit and talk to his wife. The problem is he is so crazy loud everybody can hear him. His voice carries across the whole place. Plus, that half blind old geezer can never find her grave. I always end up having to find it for him. I mean you haven't been here in years and I watched you come in and you knew right where Emily was. *Pause.* I might catch up with you later if you're still around.

CARL

Well, you got to give him a little credit. At least he's looking on the right side. He does still realize his wife was white.

CARETAKER

Very funny smart ass and before you ask. Yes, I also keep her grave site clean. Even an old white woman should have her final resting place be nice.

CARETAKER *begins to walk away and stops to turn back.*

CARETAKER (cont.)
Hey, you are going to be at the bar tonight, right?

CARL
I don't know. I might, I haven't decided yet. *Pointing.* It really depends I guess on how much of this 12 pack I have left when I'm done talking to EMZ.

CARETAKER
Alright man I'll holler at you later.

CARL *watches as* CARETAKER *walks towards* SMOKEY.

CARETAKER caringly *puts his arm on the old man's shoulder. He gently guides him to his wife's grave.*

CARL, reaches down and pulls out another beer and opens it. He then digs into his shirt pocket for his cigarettes and lights one up.

CARETAKER *walks away from* Smokey *and begins to pick up debris and placing it into his trash bag. He looks back at* CARL *and smiles.*

CARL does not notice the smile for his attention is back to EMILY.

CARL
I know you heard all that. See just like I said, what did we talk about? Baseball and softball. Then you of course. I just thought of something. I was talking about you to your friends on *Facebook.* Was that even popular when you were here? Hell, I don't even

remember. I do remember you had a *Myspace* account. I think you can still see your page. I saw it a few years back and once you're out in cyberspace you never go away. When I get home, I'm going to have to check and see. You know your old drinking buddy Smokey is here. He must be having a bad day. I guess he comes here from time to time to visit his wife.

SMOKEY'S *voice is now echoing throughout the cemetery.*

SMOKEY

How are you, my darling? How is my boy? You know I'm still trying to read that book *Catcher in the Rye* you always wanted me to read. I'm just not smart like you. I don't understand it. *Visibly shaken.* I'm just a dumb old boy from down south. How did I ever get you?

CARETAKER *drops his garbage bag and walks over to speak with him. He whispers into SMOKEY's ear and walks away. Picking up his garbage bag and exiting out the main gate.*

SMOKEY'S *voice calms.*

CARL (cont.)

Wow EMZ did you know Smokey has a son that died? I don't remember him ever saying anything to me about that. I do remember him talking about his wife, but I wouldn't have ever guessed he came out here so often. Remember, he was always looking at young girls and saying stuff? But we all know he was too old to ever try anything with them. I hope he notices I'm here before he leaves. If not, I guess I can see him at the bar tonight. If I decide to go. What if I run into that junkie ex-wife of mine? You know my famous one-week marriage. You know I don't ever tell anybody about that. My wife knows but we have been together forever at this point, so she doesn't care. But I don't tell anybody that story.

CARL *reaches over and wipes off part of the headstone. Moves the flowers closer to the middle of the grave site. He looks around for a few seconds, then turns back to focus back on* EMILY.

He reaches over and opens another beer. His empty cans are now adding up and he is lining them up in a neat row along the side of EMILY'S *grave.*

CARL (cont.)

You know the one thing that never leaves me. The one story that bothers me to this day? Was when those guys knocked that gold fish out of your hands. The one you just won at the carnival. I know they were older than we were and most likely would have kicked the living crap of me. But I still should have done what dad always said to do. Just hit the big one first and wing it from there. Just don't stop and don't ever give up. I still remember you crying when we walked home. I'm so sorry. *Sobbing.* I am just so ashamed of myself even to this day. I just can't get it out of my head. Maybe that's why I have never backed down from as fight since. Even when I knew I would lose. You know you've seen it. I don't back down from anybody. I don't care how big they are. No matter what, I still should have done something to those punks. I'm not sure if you remember, but I did get a couple of them back later? I think I was in fifth grade and you were in fourth when they tried to jump me right outside of some classroom. I don't even remember what I was doing there, but after I punched one of them. I picked the desk up outside the classroom and hit one of the other guys upside the head with it. I don't even remember what a desk was doing outside. That stopped them for a few minutes, but then I took off running. But you know there was no way they could catch me. I did see them throw a couple of coke bottle at me though. Their most likely in jail or just another dead gang member by now. I do remember that one of their older brothers was the guy the cops shot across the street from us when we lived in that upstairs apartment. You remember, that apartment that had the pool? The one that dad got drunk and started shooting from the balcony with his 12 gauge. There wasn't much of that stop sign, left, when he was done. I don't know how he got away with that one. Oh yeah, remember when the rats would crawl on the telephone wires and dad would sit outside with his 22 and shoot them. We have seen some crazy shit that's for sure.

CARL *hearing* SMOKEY'S *voice carrying throughout the cemetery again stops and glances over.*

He begins to Laugh.

CARL (cont.)

I tell you EMZ, I sure do know why you liked Smokey so much. I'm laughing just looking at him. He's over there talking to his wife. Which I know must be breaking his heart. But over here, I'm just looking at him and laughing my ass off. The way he keeps moving his arms and taking his hat on and off is funny as hell. It must just be a habit to him now. He probably couldn't stop if he wanted to.

One Drink

The fat broken machine
lay unattended.
Thighs exposed.
A darkened wild night.
The breeze moving through windows.
Passing machines cause the bushes to speak.
Tourists.
A public forest.
A missing girl.
Lights of blue and glowing.
Hunted and washed the town folk.
A bar.
One guy.
A nobody, a newcomer.
One glass continued.
The homecoming queen.
Lovely, intact.
Her dreams have turned.

Well of Hell

Growth, death.
Virtue, peace.
A pure spectacle.
A blindness replays itself.
Sorcery, the summoning.
Falling, rising.
Moments of presence.
Memories exclaiming,
chuckling.
Children new, gray.
The souls beginning.
The spirit escaped.
It's an expansion.
The darkest part of perception.
A projection.

A Rainbow in the Clouds

Eyes broken with infection.
Pout.
The prospect is red-faced,
a spectacle of atoms.
No control, divided.
The home is on fire.
No water.
Swagger is an uncertainty.
Music bows, watchful.
Not everything has vanished.
Remember to glance upwards.
Forward.
This is just an attack.
Not your home.
Masters, creatures,
are acting.
The constructive order
comes out anew.

Kingdom

Here meets a dead land,
fractured pieces,
in God's hand.
Deliberate sight,
its trembling ghost,
lands with light,
to offer the host.

Summer Months

Our configured existence
has cycles of ignorance.
Forgetful breeding succumbs,
a fallen shadow frightened.
Hiding crickets, music strums
indifferent, enlightened.
Knowledge with belligerence,
pressure begs for resistance.

New World

Foraging left-handed,
we matter.
Collected, branding,
we scatter.
The hunt for data,
discover.
In groups we adapt,
we wonder.
Clocks replace the sun,
screens are bright.
Fed, tired, bored with rain,
worship blight.

Keeper

Swear on Christ's night,
your wallet is empty,
and I may find a way
to allow you to pass.
It may kill me,
the offer will not last.

If it alludes you,
then line the sins
with new implications
so, they may live.
Denying this temptation,
cannot forgive.

Find the Time

Study the marvelous regime
of unfettered distance.
Use the night with a radio.
Believe your fur is hard.
The shield will break.
Tamed by mention.
How deep will you ask?
What occurrences
provided your conscience?
Did a curve and string dream
shatter your slumber?
Welcome to the event
of rejected destinies.

Little Sister

A figure walks through a dark, empty house. The moonlight is a guide, the tiny hands pan the wall. He knows the house well.

The power is out. The switch is useless.

There is a faint sound of sobbing. Nobody is there to hear it.

An old man, a bedroom window, and a glass of whisky resting on the windowsill.

A little boy walks towards the front door. Pausing, he looks into the junk car in the driveway.

Remember, say nothing or you'll
be in real trouble. Now go to sleep.

An evil grin.

Shush!!

The sun is up and his hands shake as he pours bourbon into his coffee. He attempts to light a cigarette.

BAM... A gunshot.

Let go of it, let it go. Drop the gun.

Children run from their rooms.

Get back in your rooms! All of you, now!

Calmly.

We are going to tell the police he did this
to himself. Do you understand?
Yeah.
Now go wash up and make sure
you wash your hands really good,
and use lots of soap.

The paramedics wheel a body from the house.

Why would he want to kill himself?
He was a worthless drunk.
Where did the gun come from?
I don't know, he had it for years.
You don't exactly seem to be very upset.
I'm not.

Ley Lines

Have we failed the stars
whom influence us?
The innocence of our beginning?
Before us stretches our regret.
Wrecked, not regaled
by the warfare exploding.
We urge our gods for thunder.
With it our delight
for our children.
A realm of water and supported gates.
Order the blood from the pigs lurking.
Sentence the destructor.
And pray among the plum fields.
Let us then dance with the artists.
Signal the spending
of celestial inspiration.
Continue with us
and declare the pastels
of our torches will not fade.
Support the spirits
of the thicket dwellers.
Show us the way.
The way of our forefathers'
sacred canoes.
Lay routes upon the public seas.
Examine us as we traverse.
Hold our hand to clean the earth.

Hero

Appropriate, the stars.
Appearance fulfills irony.
The brightness
rebukes any miscalculation.
Their presence
justifies the mortal properties.
It spit us as debris.
Never knowing
it conceived a youth.
Through the fire
which heats my night.
My nature.
I attend to its grandeur.
I inhale its donation.
I lay.
I study.

Hamilton Porter

He was an extensive fellow.
Smoothness drained from him.
Crumbs showered the field
as he strode.
He held an unhurried hand.
Executed with rigor.
His sweep left a pathway.
An orientation to follow.
Youngsters perched on balconies,
recognizing the periods of being
locked in the basement.
His absence leaves a maiming.
The gate of precision
now murmurs, secluded.
His fretful tear rubbed away.
The journey was heading west.

Zip Gun

Tutor on the asphalt.
There were butcher shops,
ball games on the radio.
Fights are children growing.
T-shirts and Levi's.
Magazines, picture dictionaries
for the youthful.
Stolen cigarettes.
Bars are where the heroes live.
Stolen cars and childhoods.
Young woman, not a queen.
Friends more influential
than the household.
Neighborhoods explained you.
Falling out, tough.
Falling in had not begun.

Dutch

Patriots struggled
for these timbers.
Hallowed, the laurel path
of liberation flourished.
Unique are the views
of circumstance.
The whisper of woe
carries this wonderful river.
Shining in its coma.

Hushed, the sun's perfume
is a yellow butterfly.
It floats the delicacy of a fresh course.
Red, white and black,
the colors continue tall.
The surrendering has emerged.
My gaze ends with its charm.
Stunned by the palm resting on mine.
It is bliss.

Semitae

With a glowing gaze,
stationary.
A skeleton of youth
produces its mark,
an outline
on the heated canvas.

As a ravenous artist,
the clouds avoid the west.
In a man-made container,
the primitive gambol and splash.
The voices of this feast
are spun, forever young.

Me, you and you

Three stages, the declaration bounced. A youthful man drifts in and announced. His make is for me, you and you. Where he maintains, nobody knew. The vast flat boat moves slow. Its four-year glory. Became a generation long story. Glittering the odd tune, walked. Staggering, he understood his talk. He studied his left from his right. From creation, determined to fight. He gawked at the light. To keep away the night.

Life killed the fringes of his cap. Now gray, he judges during his nap. Only scratching's stay complete. Their great grandchildren, they will never meet. Days will sail by, and identities will die. Stories become fuller, and offspring will lie. A picture dabbles with the dove. A glimpse will move the distance of love.

No Consecutive Road

Is it luck or an arduous thought, maybe the purpose of God? We position allure, figure where it sits. Man's readiness to accept chances measures distance. How meaningful can he disappear? He's stretched out among the luminary. Paused at the other side. And picked up the account of both God and devil. There is no consecutive road. No proper part, nor serious side. There is no abuse in observing walls producing hair. The tone of the design crackling lasts a life. People should adopt the visions, grasp them, spread them, snuggle them when you are alone. Giggle with them when stoned.

The Hike - A True Story (Lockwood Canyon Trail)

Off in the distance the sound of gun shots.

Coming around the final corner of their hike, walking on a downward slope the trio is have a smile on their face.

> *There it is, the car, our savior.*
> *Give me a break, it's only been two and* half hours
> *That's a long time in the sun mom.*

Something suddenly catches their eye. A pile of rocks is stacked under the sage brush.

> Come with me.
>
> *Where?*
>
> *There, the pile of rocks?*
>
> *What about it?*
>
> *Look at that, there is no way that is natural. Somebody stacked them like that for a reason.*

They begin to move the rocks.

Don't do that. It's probably just someone's dog or something. I don't want to see any dog bones.

Look at this. It's no dog. If this is drugs we are fucked cause someone is coming to get this.

Why would they put drugs out here?

I don't know, but meth heads aren't exactly known for their IQ's. It might actually, be a good idea if it's done at the right time of day. Just not now when people are walking the trail. Let's just put it back and get the fuck out of here.

Look, there is a note or something in the bag. Don't you see it?

What's does it say?

"This package contains the incinerated Remains of Samuel D. Whitman, age 78 years. Born April 16,1931 and died on January 12,2010 and whose body was cremated on the above first mentioned date at the Masonic Memorial Gardens crematory"

Holy shit, dad just fingered a dead guy.

The Old Painted Rose

You have exhaled,
unbroken,
through sharp rains,
life strains.
Equipped,
a consciousness,
a tempted venture.
You will never wither,
the rarest treasure.
Buried,
a decorating bed.
Glorious,
the greater pleasure.

The Purge

Hell purged,
and death
sprinkled its dust.
Men tumbled
from the skies;
battles roared with a grin.
Fathers advanced
against their children.
Courts condemned the free,
fixed the sly on thrones.
The earth drowned
in the mention of liberation.

Gut Feeling

Never dread the relationship.
The path of your awareness
is infinite.
Steering,
it gives bearing.
Durable, tall
or trembling,
relaxing can place you.
Once lost,
or on the side
of the road.
Like an old car,
it smacks.
It reaches your gut,
and ransacks.
Turn left,
then turn left,
then turn left,
then turn left....

Shelter

Strangled,
the shelter had wheels.
Fog the alarm clock.
An excruciating birth.
Introducing the term
of affection.
How ill is life?
A child vaults
over the gorge.
The blackness
is on the other side.
Fancies reversed;
the individual slept.
No sharp period
to arrest the craving.
He now lives
in Mark Twain's dwelling.

Tickles

My minister's order is diligent.
He never plucked a revolver
he didn't aim to use.
A ridiculous fellow, weighs
but cannot resolve.
It's a frigid father
who will hover.
He roars at the animal quality;
the blood tickles his ear.

An Old Connecticut Home

He presents not to know
everything nor does he see it.
A court composer tossed, invaded.
The processes
surround the skeletons.
In his preceding existence,
they delivered him
to this extraordinary sight.
Watching the trees carry
color from year to death.
It will be here
he takes his last breath.

Derived From an English Name

The display is obvious
in this remarkable business.
A fascinating window,
bright with conjecture.
I am better composed
with an addict
than a millionaire.
I am the best artist
with an addict
millionaire.

Culminate

An essential incident
is a weapon of decision.
Decades are infamous
in a moment.
A glance foreshadows
the end.
Count backwards.
See the question.
What is the plot
of this story?

Times

Abolition blooms to be.
The strength of man as he
In bothered moments,
The sun's opponent
Begs the gratitude,
Freedom's solitude.
Questioning others
Once your brothers,
The past does not forget
You, it will not let.

A Bat in the Flue

Beat, stale. I request sleep.
I carried long, God
has positioned me.
They discarded the fronds.
A tick's infection is weak
Exodus is but an antique.
I request sleep.

Warm, I submerge.
It is my place, this intention
released me passionately.
Voiced wind brushed
this time's approval.
Shortly will be my removal.
I request sleep.

www.ingramcontent.com/pod-product-compliance
Lightning Source LLC
Chambersburg PA
CBHW050024170726
48282CB00025B/533

* 9 7 8 8 1 8 2 5 3 8 9 4 8 *